THE

·303 LEWIS GUN

by

Capt. G. JACKLIN

and

DEREK WHIPP

Illustrated by

R. BARNARD WAY

The Naval & Military Press Ltd

Published by

The Naval & Military Press Ltd

Unit 5 Riverside, Brambleside
Bellbrook Industrial Estate
Uckfield, East Sussex
TN22 1QQ England

Tel: +44 (0)1825 749494

www.naval-military-press.com
www.nmarchive.com

THE ·303 LEWIS GUN

CAN your fingers see better than your eyes?

Because to be a first-class Lewis gunner, your fingers will need to be trained to such a pitch of sensitivity that you know exactly what part of the gun you are holding and precisely where it fits.

You must develop eyes in your finger-tips—eyes capable of seeing as well by night as by day.

MEET THE GUN

THE Lewis .303 Light Automatic, to call it by its proper name, is a beautiful job, but unless you take enthusiastically to the task of learning all about it right from the start, you will have difficulty in qualifying.

Still, you must be interested, or else you would not have bothered to pick up this book. The matter it contains is no love story. It is the other extreme!

Your reaction as a potential but inexperienced Lewis gunner will doubtless be to learn all about holding down the trigger and letting rip. Unfortunately, it is not so easy as that. In fact, the .303 Lewis should be fired in bursts of four or five rounds at the most, and never until the target is sufficiently large and vulnerable. By using it haphazardly, its position would be disclosed to the enemy and its effectiveness destroyed.

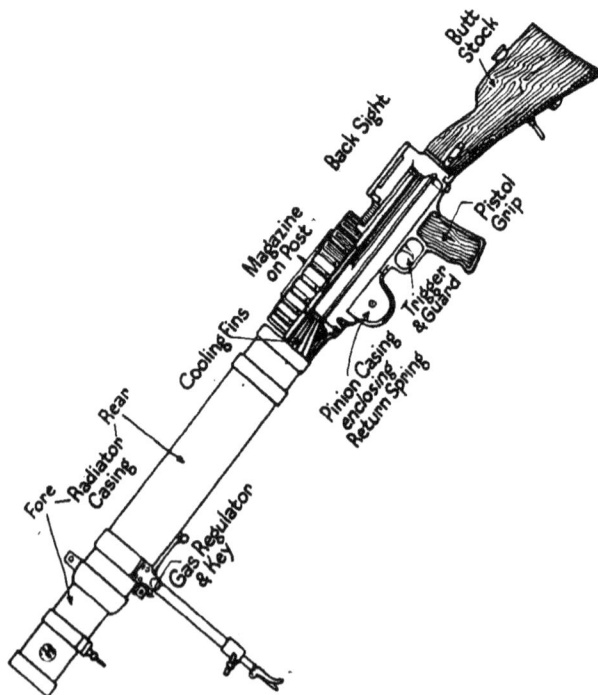

So take your finger off the trigger for a while and get to know something about the gun before you have wiped out the whole of the German Army.

Here are seven points about the .303 Lewis which make it such a deadly weapon:

1. Weight, about 27 lbs. . . . easy to carry.

2. Compactness . . . offering small target to enemy.

3. Operators—one firer, one loader . . . firing
   capacity equal to at least 50 riflemen.

4. Rapid gun-laying . . . 50 riflemen shifting to
   alternative target would make considerable
   movement, and would not move so quickly.

5. Rate of fire, 600 rounds per minute . . . paralysing effect on enemy.

6. Muzzle velocity, 2,460 feet per second . . . used
   intelligently, the opposition is wiped out
   before getting a chance to reply.

7. Range, 1,900 yards.

CHARACTERISTICS

AUTOMATIC weapons work on basically the same principle . . . the expansion of gases has the effect of pushing back the cocking action as well as expelling the bullet, and some form of spring is responsible for the forward action by which the explosive is detonated.

With the .303 Lewis, the gas pressure is about 19 tons per square inch, and this force is used also in the cooling system . . . but that will be dealt with later.

Air cools the barrel, and the magazines, which can hold 47 rounds, feed this hungry brute. A full magazine weighs 4½ lbs., and empty 1½ lbs.

LET'S LOOK INSIDE

To develop those eyes at your finger-tips, you should practise stripping and examining and naming and, most particularly, knowing by touch every part of the gun, until you can do it automatically—even when blindfold.

The gun has two main parts: the Body Group and the Barrel Group. The best way of learning is to get a good knowledge of the Body Group first.

Every Lewis gunner in the British Army knows the gun inside and out, and to stress the importance of seeking that standard, I'll tell you soon of a true incident which immobilised six of thirteen guns, purely because the men were poorly trained.

The Lewis is made so that nearly all the main parts can be stripped with nothing more elaborate than the nose of a round.

Don't hurry with the stripping or assembling in the early stages. You might easily damage some vital part. Not you, particularly. But it has been done—and only because the novice was more enthusiastic than slick.

When stripping, get into the habit of placing the mechanism upwards in a clean, dry spot.

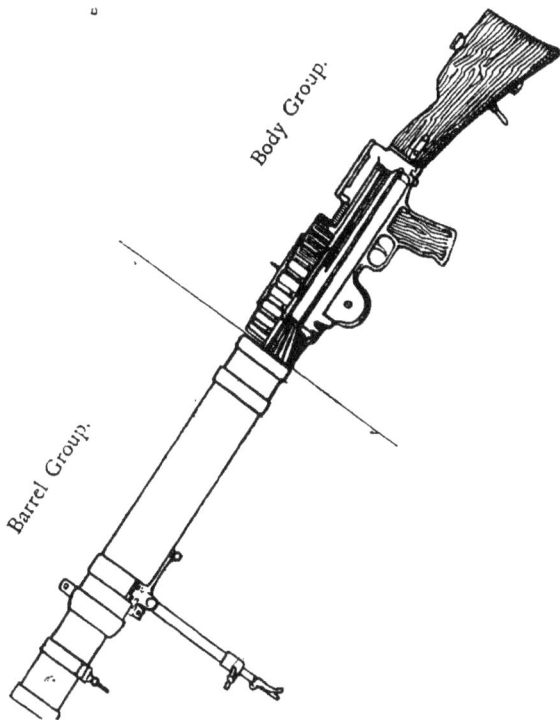

Now we'll open it up, and if you can appreciate machine precision, the inside will call for your admiration.

Don't try to read the matter from this point without following it with a gun in front of you.

SEQUENCE

HERE is the sequence in which you should strip:

(1) Always feel or see that the *Cocking Handle* is in the forward position before you start. With the nose of a bullet or the thumb of the left hand, press

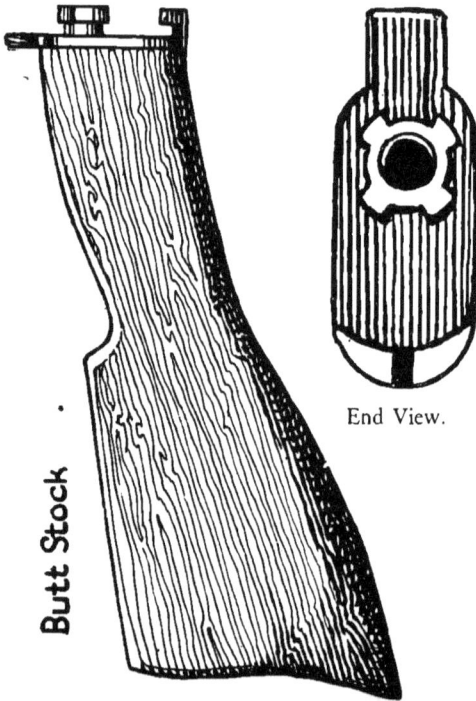

End View.

Butt Stock

forward the butt catch which you will find just underneath the rear end of the *Body*, and with the right hand rotate enough to free the *Butt* so that it comes away from the body.

(2) Now the *Body Cover*. The middle finger of each hand is placed in front of the body cover and behind the tongue. The thumbs are placed below it and on the body near where the butt was before you

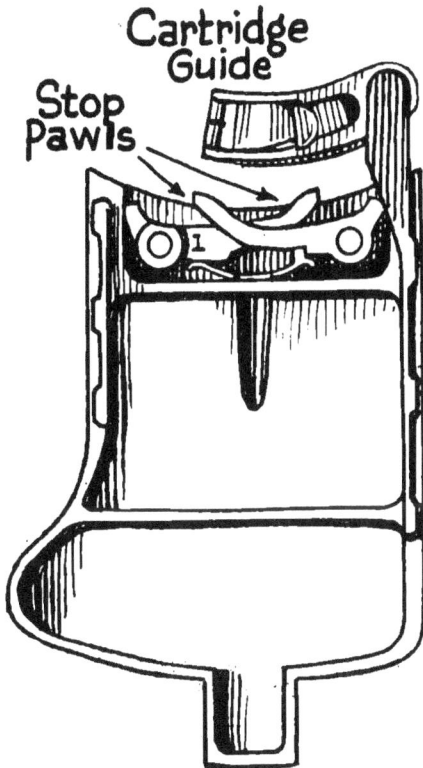

Under Side of Body Cover.

took it off. Press back the locking lugs, and the body slides backwards and off.

Well, well. Six paragraphs ago, the importance of placing the mechanism *upwards* was stressed. It's strange how many people make the mistake of placing the body cover downwards the first time they remove it.

(3) The *Feed Arm*. A bullet nose will help to

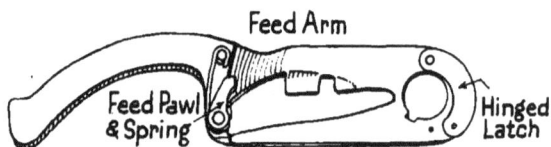

push forward the latch which holds the Feed Arm in position on the magazine post. Lift the rear end of the Feed Arm to the right until the keyway comes

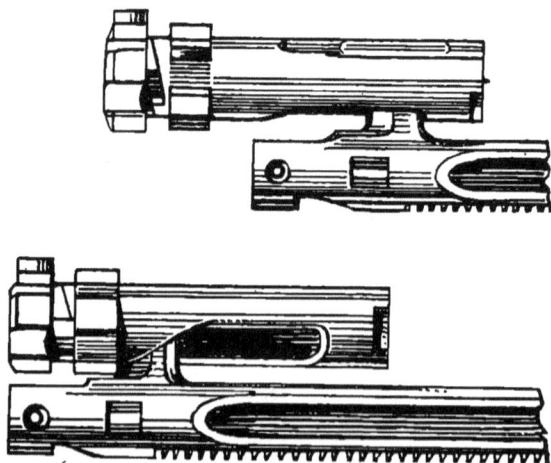

Bolt and End of Piston Rod.

opposite the key on the magazine post. Lift off and close the latch, then disconnect by pressing back the trigger and pulling back the pistol grip far enough to allow the *Pinion Group* to hang down on its hinge.

The *Bolt* and *Piston Rod* are now removed by first
drawing back the cocking handle to its full extent

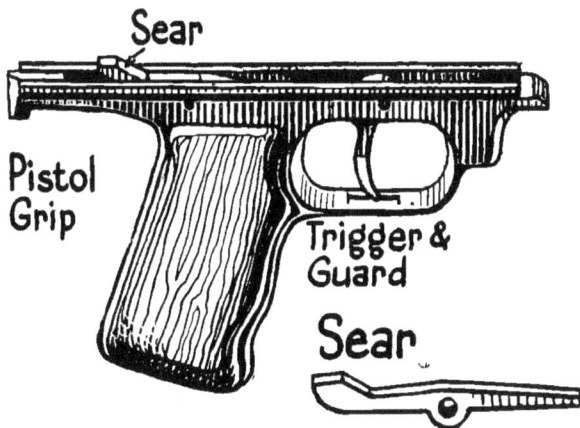

and pulling out. Don't yank out the piston rod all
the way and look surprised when the bolt clatters to
the ground. Place the fingers in front of the bolt
and slide it towards you and lift it off the striker post

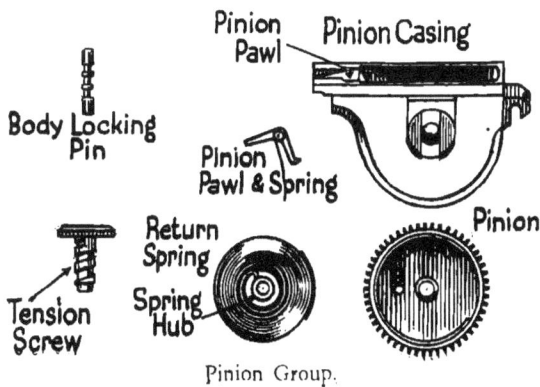

Pinion Group.

as soon as it clears the body. You can then remove the piston rod, but take a fresh grip on the flexible joint when removing the piston rod.

Only three more items, and you have stripped the main parts of the Body Group.

(4) The *Pistol Grip* is drawn back until the retaining rails are clear of the body. And if the novice still hasn't learnt his lesson, he promptly turns it upside down and plonks it in a nice muddy puddle.

(5) Next, remove the pinion by lifting the claw from the hinge. In front of this hinge, you will find the body locking pin which is dug out by the nose of a round.

(6) Finally, rotate the body to the left until it is free of the barrel.

TO ASSEMBLE

You have now stripped the main parts of the body group, but that's nothing to what you still have to learn. The best way to absorb the matter so far dealt with is to reverse the sequence and name and feel these parts as you put them back.

We'll run through the assembling together very briefly.

(1) Replace the body on the barrel, press home and turn, making sure by rubbing the thumb over the joint that the body is flush with the magazine platform.

(2) Restore the body locking pin and hang the pinion group on the hinge, then, to assist in

assembling, replace the pistol grip, but do not connect.

(3) Next come the piston rod and bolt. The piston rod is inserted into the body until the striker is about

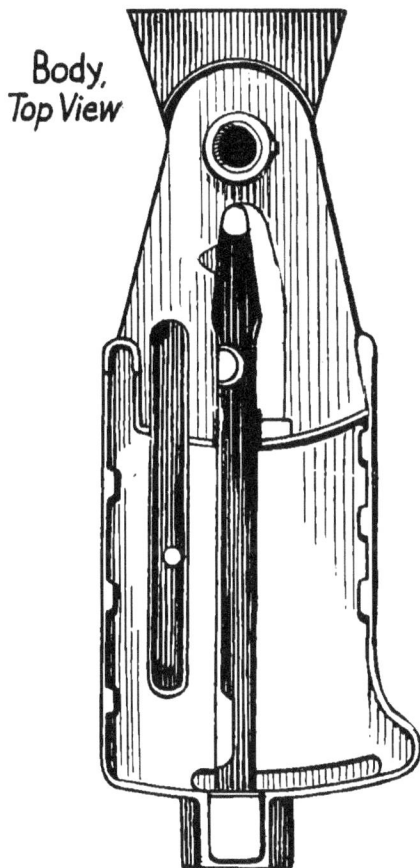

Body,
Top View

eight inches from the rear end. The bolt is placed on the piston rod, and at this stage it is as well to make sure that the actuating stud is fully home.

The bolt is now pushed forward AND NOT THE PISTON ROD until the rear end of the actuating stud is flush with the end of the body. Insert the cocking handle and push fully home. Advance the cocking handle until it can go no further, and if you can pull it out when it is in the forward position, you will have to bring it back and *try again, remembering to push it home properly this time.*

Magazine Post.

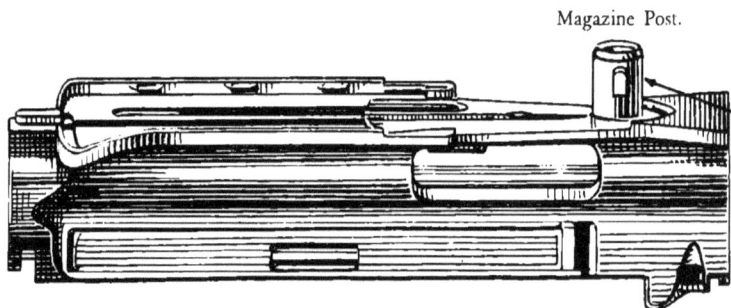

Body Side View.

To connect the pistol grip to the pinion group, hold up the latter with the fingers of the left hand, thumb on top of the body as tightly as possible, press the trigger and force the pistol grip forward until the pinion group is engaged. The feed arm has to be put back after this, so open the latch, place it on the magazine post, and shift until the keyway is opposite the key. After the feed arm has fallen into its place, close the latch and engage the undercut tail on the heart-shaped boss on the actuating stud. Always make sure that the feed arm is to the right when assembling.

The body cover, held in the same grip as when stripping, is placed on the body about half an inch behind its normal position, so that the interruptions clear the flanges. Tap forward sharply, assuring yourself afterwards that the edges are flush with the edges of the body. Replace the butt by inserting the locking lugs into the recesses and twisting to the correct position.

You can't get the butt back? Then either the body cover or the pistol grip hasn't been pushed far enough forward.

THE BARREL GROUP

To STRIP: Using that indispensable bullet nose again, lift the rear end of the gas regulator key from its seat and rotate either way and remove from the gas regulator. Unscrew the bipod clamp ring and take off the front radiator casing. Holding the exposed part of the radiator centre, pull off the rear of the radiator casing. To remove the gas cylinder, insert the piston until the rack is engaged on the flat part, rotate to the left, unscrew and remove.

Get the spanner from the spare parts kit and unscrew the barrel mouthpiece, REMEMBERING THAT IT SHIFTS FROM RIGHT TO LEFT. The reason for this left-hand thread is that the barrel rifling is from left

to right, and the action of firing might easily unscrew
the mouthpiece at an awkward moment.

The spanner is used also to unscrew the gas
chamber, which is then removed from its seating in
the barrel.

To Reassemble : Reverse the order. This is the
sequence, numbered for brevity : (1) Barrel mouthpiece. (2) Gas chamber. (3) Gas cylinder. (4) Rear
end radiator casing. (5) Fore end radiator casing.
(6) Clamp ring. (7) Gas regulator key.

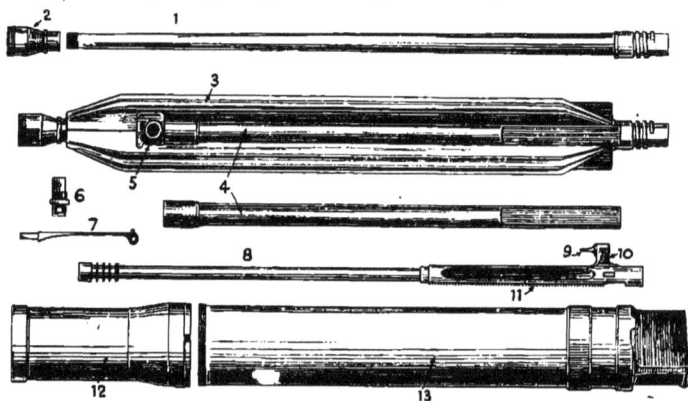

1. Barrel. 2. Barrel Mouthpiece. 3. Radiator (underside view).
4. Gas Cylinder. 5. Gas Chamber. 6. Gas Regulator. 7. Gas
Regulator Key. 8. Piston Rod showing Cup, Rings Rack, Bent
Striker Post and Striker. 9. Striker. 10. Striker Post. 11. Rack.
12. Fore Radiator Casing. 13. Rear Radiator Casing.

An important point here is that the barrel register
(the lip at the end of the barrel that regulates the
amount of cartridge to be gripped by the extractor) is
the most delicate part of the gun. Take every care
that it is not damaged.

THE BITS YOU HANDLED

You have now stripped and reassembled both main parts. With practice, it will become second nature, and you won't be puzzling your brain about which bit goes back where.

We'll run over the parts, and give a bit more detail about them, stripping as we do so. Try to remember the names, but more important, get the *feel* firmly implanted.

THE BUTT.—Those knobbly bits which attach the butt to the body are called the cruciform locking lugs. Below these is a recess into which the butt catch fits.

End View

And the flat bit between the locking lugs and the butt catch acts as a stop for the bolt and pistol. This is called the tang.

THE BODY COVER.—At the front there is a projecting tongue which is undercut to take the cartridge guide. A hole in the tongue holds in place a positioning stud on the cartridge guide. The cartridge guide is so shaped and placed that as the bolt travels forward, the round is prevented from rising. Immediately behind are the axis studs for the stop pawls, numbered 1 and 2.

If you remember that No. 2 has a clubbed head and always goes on the right, you won't make the mistake which earlier I promised to tell you about.

Soon after the Great War, I was serving in another country with some poorly trained troops, and was detailed to inspect the guns of a certain Command.

Cartridge Guide.

Stop Pawls Spring

No 1 Stop Pawl Left

No 2 Stop Pawl Right

Out of thirteen, I found that six had been put aside as useless. The only thing wrong was that the pawls had been replaced in the reverse order. This could never happen in the British Army, because the men are so thoroughly trained.

The pawls are kept in position by a butterfly spring called the stop pawl spring held by a stud fitting into a hole in the rib of the body. A lip on the spring engages the right stop pawl, and the body cover, locked by flanges and projections, is ridged underneath to prevent upward movement of the feed arm.

TANGENT SIGHT.—At the butt end, you will find the tangent sight. It is dovetailed to the top of the body cover and consists of the leaf, fixed by a washer and split pin, and slide variable by a milled-head screw for sighting up to 1,900 yards. The tangent sight spring assists in the movement of this main part.

FEED ARM.—The front of the feed arm has a hole so shaped that it will pass over the magazine post and in one position over the magazine key. It is secured to the magazine post by a hinged latch. A slot called

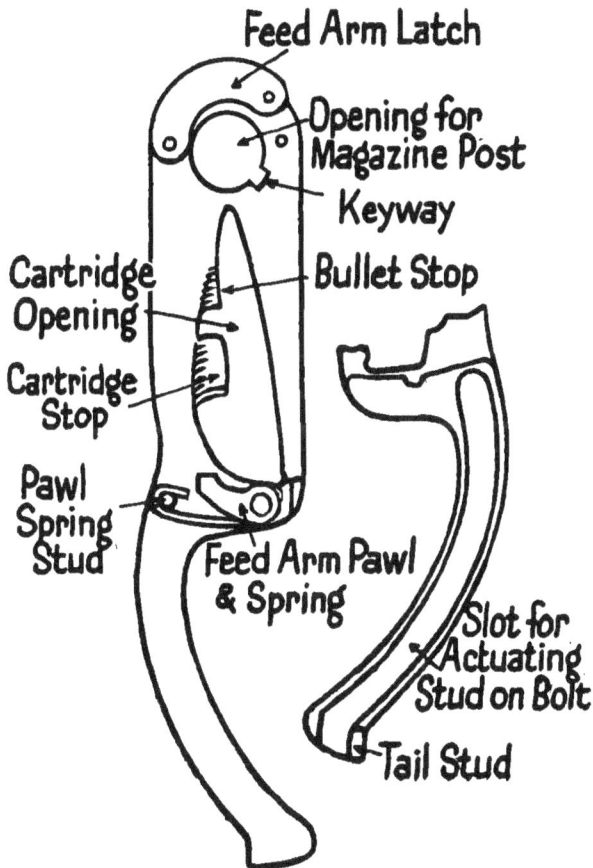

Feed Arm Latch

Opening for Magazine Post

Keyway

Cartridge Opening

Bullet Stop

Cartridge Stop

Pawl Spring Stud

Feed Arm Pawl & Spring

Slot for Actuating Stud on Bolt

Tail Stud

the cartridge way is cut in the front end, allowing cartridges to fall from the magazine on to the body.

The left of the cartridge way has a clearance for the separating pegs of the magazine, the top right corner of which is shaped to feed the bullet into the breach. A tongue behind the clearance prevents the

Bolt

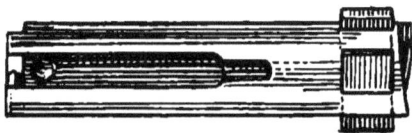

Extractor

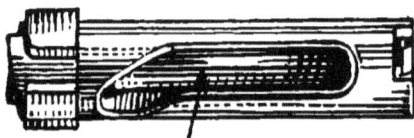

Bolt, showing Cam Slot

cartridge from rising when clear of the cartridge guide spring.

Three studs will be found further down the feed arm—the feed pawl stud, feed pawl spring stud and feed pawl retaining stud. The feed pawl works on a fish-hook spring kept in position by a small stud on its underside, the pawl being slotted to take the spring. The pawl stud acts as an axis pin for the feed pawl and the feed pawl stop stud has a restraining influence on the feed pawl in its urge to move forward. The feed arm's tail is grooved to accommodate the boss of the actuating stud. The end of the tail has a stud which limits the amount of lateral movement on top of the body.

THE BOLT.—On the face of the bolt is the Striker Way. It is grooved to take the base of the cartridge and slots are cut for the head of the ejector and the

Feed Arm Actuating Stud

empty cases, also to take the extractors which are sprung into the side of the bolt. The extractors are flat springs with claws which fit round the rim of the cartridge. A stud sprung into the end of the bolt keeps them in position. There is a cammed slot in the bolt which locks the bolt for the distance before the cam until the round is fired. Four lugs at the rear end of the bolt lock it to the body and the left locking lug is cut away slightly to allow the tail of the ejector to ride over it in the forward action. The screw thread on the rear end of the bolt takes the external threads on the actuating stud.

THE ACTUATING STUD.—Of the four guide lugs which travel along the guide ways in the rear of the body, that which seems to do the most important work is that heart-shaped one which fits into the tail of the feed arm, causing lateral movement in the feed arm. But they're all important in the construction of the gun.

THE PISTON ROD.—The flexible joint in the piston rod divides the two solid pieces of steel. Fixed by a pin, the flexible joint acts as a slight shock absorber after the gases have forced back the piston rod. Damage might be caused if the piston rod, in absolute solid form, were to crash to the rear of the gun with every re-cocking. The piston has a cup-shaped head and four rings to trap any gases which escape over the cup. Under the rear portion of the piston is the rack, and at the butt end you will find a small hollow square, cut at the front end into which

Sear

Piston Rod.
showing Cup,
Rings, Rack,
Bent Striker
Post and
Striker.

fits the nose of the sear. This is just above the slot which receives the cocking handle. The rear end of the piston rod is bored to take the nose of a bullet to help shifting if the cocking handle is lost. The striker post and striker, also at the butt end of the piston rod, are worth your attention. The striker is kept in position by a pin, and the striker post is chamfered or cut away on its left front and right rear.

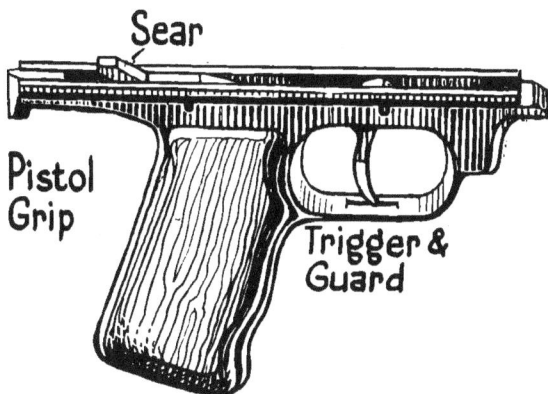

PISTOL GRIP.—This is made up of a holding for the thumb, second, third and fourth fingers of the right hand, the plunger, the trigger, the sear and the butt catch. The plunger fits into the front end, actuating both the pinion pawl and the nose of the sear when the trigger is depressed.

THE SEAR AND TRIGGER.—The trigger transmits movement to the sear through a knuckle joint. When receiving Lewis gun training in the early stages of the last war, we used to recite this couplet:

'On pressing the trigger, the nose of the sear
   Becomes disengaged from the bent in the rack.
Very doggerel, admittedly, but we used to con-

tinue: thus allowing the return spring to carry forward the piston rod and bolt.

If you can succeed in putting in rhyme the complete Lewis gun training, your efforts may be rewarded by a decoration—or perhaps just the soft-spoken gratitude of fellows whose enthusiasm flagged as they waded through what is admittedly a highly technical affair.

THE PINION GROUP has a casing, the pinion, the return spring, the **T**-shaped tension screw, hub,

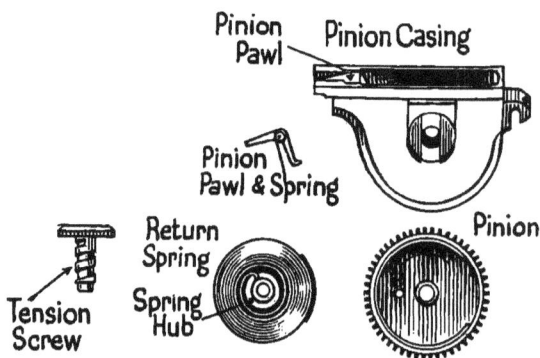

pinion pawl, and pinion pawl spring. The front end of the casing has a claw which holds it by the hinge to the front end of the body, and at the rear end of the casing is the pinion pawl which is worked by a spring. This keeps the spring tense when the pinion is removed from the gun. The return spring and pinion are kept in position by the **T**-shaped tension screw which enters the casing from the right side. The pinion teeth fit into the teeth of the rack and the return spring is held in the casing which has a slot corresponding with slots on the inside of the case. That is so that it cannot be put in back to front. One end of the return spring is leaded to enter the slot in the hub, and the hub is bored and screwed to take the T-shaped tension screw.

THE BODY.—The front of the body is threaded to receive the barrel and bored for the piston rod and body locking pin. The groove on the right side is to shift the body locking pin. The bottom of the body is recessed to allow the pinion plunger and sear to operate. At the front of this recess is the pinion claw hinge. A slow is cut for the cocking handle in its backward and forward movement, and underneath the body are the rails which correspond with the rails on the pistol grip. On the right side of the body is the ejection opening. The magazine post, which is at the top front of the body, has a small key on its right side to hold the centre part of the magazine, while the outer part—that containing the cartridges—rotates and expels the ammunition which drops into place. The top of the body is cut and shaped to take the cartridge and the boss on the actuating stud. The small depression to the left front of the cartridge way takes the bullet stop on the feed arm and a groove at the rear end takes the base of the round.

On the left and in the rear is the ejector seating which is enclosed by a spring cover. There is a recess at the rear end of the body which takes the stud on the extreme end of the feed arm. The body is bored to take the bolt and piston and the bolt way is grooved with four guide ways recessed at the rear to take the locking lugs on the butt. At the front end of the bolt way are the locking recesses which accommodate the locking lugs and bolt when the action is forward. On the left side of the bolt way are slots cut which allow the head and tail of the ejector alternately to project into the bolt way. The piston way is cut to receive the rack.

THE BARREL GROUP

THE GAS REGULATOR AND KEY.—The gas regulator key is shaped to fit into the gas regulator, being held

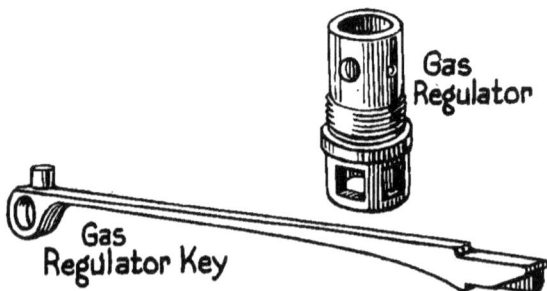

in position by the stud engaging in the small hole in the rear radiator casing. The gas regulator screws into the gas chamber and has two holes marked L and S. Normally, the small hole should be opposite the gas chamber hole. It is held in position by the gas regulator key.

THE RADIATOR CASING has two parts, the fore and rear ends, and is dulled to prevent reflection of light. The two parts are kept in position by the clamp ring, the front portion being narrowed at its extreme end to assist in the action of the gases. The rear portion protects the aluminium radiator. It is bored and drilled to take the gas regulator and the stud on the gas regulator key, the gas regulator, the barrel, the gas cylinder, and the body locking pin. Slots at the front end correspond with slots on the fore part of the radiator casing to take the positioning stud on the clamp ring. The gas cylinder is a long tube, the rounded end of which is threaded to take the gas chamber while the other end is flattened to take the rack on the piston.

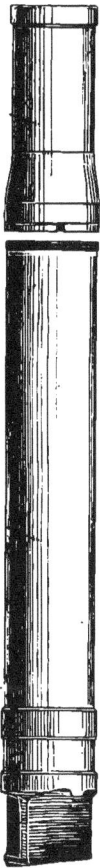

Fore and Rear Radiator Casing.

Gas Cylinder.

THE GAS CHAMBER.—The nipple of the gas chamber is threaded internally to take the barrel band and externally to receive the gas cylinder. Two wings act as a grip for the mouthpiece spanner.

The ends of the clamp ring are turned up and out

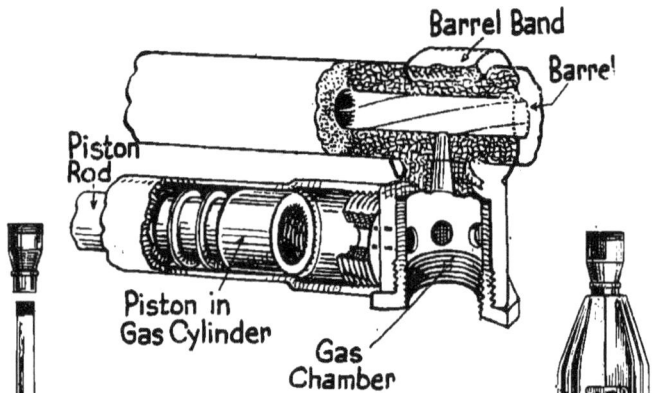

Barrel Band

Barrel

Piston Rod

Piston in Gas Cylinder

Gas Chamber

Barrel and Mouthpiece.

to protect the foresight. The inside part of the right protector is dovetailed to receive the foresight and acts as a plug, being held in position by a screw which must always be placed on the gun to the right.

THE RADIATOR.—Made of aluminium for lightness, the radiator is sprung on to the barrel and so shaped that a continuous stream of cool air will pass through its seventeen fins from the rear to the front when the gun is fired. It is recessed to take the gas chamber

Radiator, Underside View.

and cylinder. The barrel band fits over the gas vent and is threaded to take the gas chamber nipple.

THE BARREL MOUTHPIECE has a left-handed thread which holds it on to the muzzle end of the barrel. It is so shaped that it helps in the cooling action of the gun and also keeps the radiator in position on the barrel.

LOADING, FIRING AND UNLOADING

LOADING.—Before you can fire, the magazine has to be fitted on to the magazine post with the thumb catch to the right. Press the magazine fully home and rotate by drawing the palm of your right hand towards you and continue to do so until resistance is felt. Pull back the cocking handle to its fullest extent and the first round, held under the cartridge guide in the feedway, is now ready to be fired.

You can't move the cocking handle? Perhaps it is as well. The safety catch was applied by the chap who used the gun last, and it may be useful as a lesson to you that the first thing you do before loading is to see that the cocking handle is in the forward position.

FIRING.—The purpose of any gun is to do most damage with the least possible expenditure of ammunition, and to get the maximum fire effect from the Lewis it is essential that the gun should be relaid after every four or five rounds. This is because with most automatics the action causes jumping, and the aiming mark is not maintained. A rifleman has to sight each shot, but by the time the last of a short burst from the Lewis has left the barrel, the gunner cannot be sure he is still on the mark. The trained Lewis gunner remembers the value of short bursts, so when you go on the open range and have a full magazine on your gun, try to remember this.

The firing action is carried out in the following sequence: aim, press, release, observe. And if there's no enemy about, pack up and save your ammunition.

Aiming is similar to any weapon fitted with the aperture backsight and blade foresight; that is, the tip of the foresight is in the centre of the aperture and that combination of sights is directed at six o'clock or the lowest central portion of the aiming mark.

UNLOADING.—There are two methods of unloading —the normal and the abnormal. Normally, the magazine is removed, the butt held in the shoulder and the bullet fired at a point where no harm can be done.

The abnormal method is used when the gunner does not want to disclose his location. Remove the magazine, and with the forefinger of the left hand ease down the base of the round held in the feedway until the nose of the bullet appears above the cartridge way. The right hand now grips the nose of the round and eases it forward until it rests on the feed arm. Now grab the cocking handle with the right hand, press the trigger with the left hand and move the cocking handle backwards and forward UNDER CONTROL until the round is clear of the feedway. It's no good realising how clumsy you are after you have let the cocking handle slip out of your grasp, causing the round to be discharged.

When the round has cleared the feedway, remove from the top of the body and press the trigger.

HOW IT WORKS

WHEN a round is fired, the bullet is pushed up the barrel by the gas caused by the explosion. Part of this gas passes through the gas port and into the gas

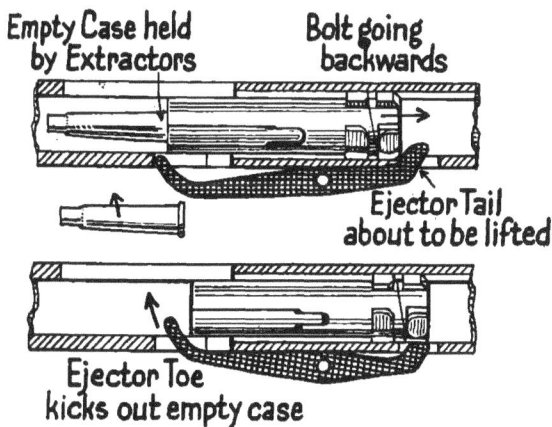

Ejection Mechanism.

chamber, thence to the gas regulator, and from there via one of the two small holes in the regulator to the gas cylinder. Here it strikes the cup-shaped head of the piston and forces it violently to the rear, rewinding the return spring because the rack is engaged in the pinion teeth.

Before the bolt can be unlocked, the striker travels backwards about 1¼ inches down the straight part of the cammed slot. Then the right side of the striker post bearing against the right curved part of the cammed slot rotates the bolt from right to left, thus releasing the locking lugs from the locking recesses.

As the bolt moves backwards the extractors withdraw the empty case from the chamber and the left guide lug on the actuating stud strikes the tail of the ejector which is on the pivot. This forces the head

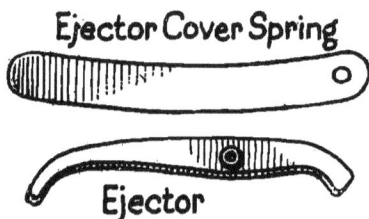

Ejector Cover Spring

Ejector

of the ejector across the face of the bolt where it strikes the empty case and forces it through the opening on the right side of the body. At the same time, the boss on the actuating stud, being engaged in the curved tail of the feed arm, carries the feed arm from right to left. The feed pawl, being engaged behind the corrugation of the magazine, carries the magazine one space in the feeding direction.

As the magazine rotates, the corrugation passes over the face of the left stop pawl and depresses it, rising again and engaging behind the corrugation. This stops rebound. The feed pawl spring stud, riding away from the face of the right stop pawl, allows it to spring forward and engage in front of the corrugation, stopping the magazine from rotating too far in the feeding direction.

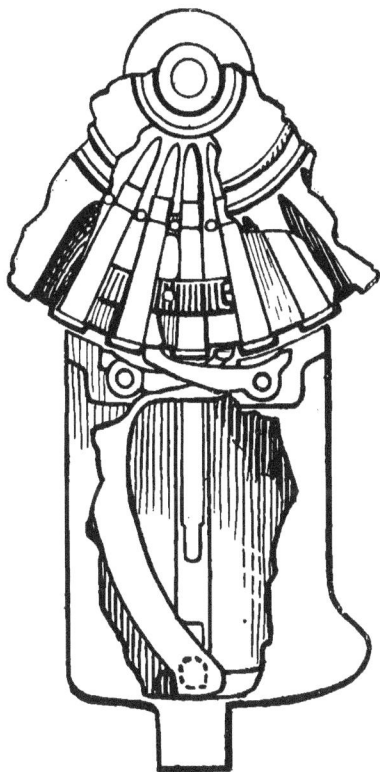

Sectional View of Magazine Feed. 1st Action.

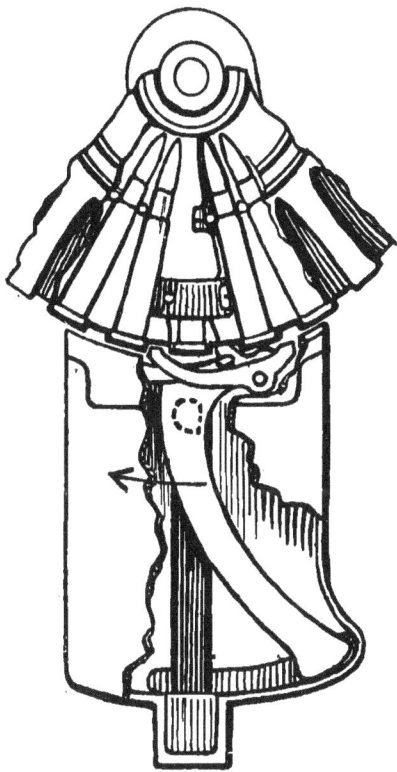

Sectional View of Magazine Feed. 2nd Action.

The pawl and the piston rod continue to travel to the rear, where they hit the butt tang, and the force of the gas is expended.

THE FEEDING ACTION

As the magazine rotates, the cartridges are carried round the centre block by means of the separating

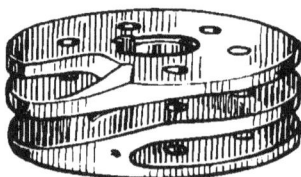

Centre Block.

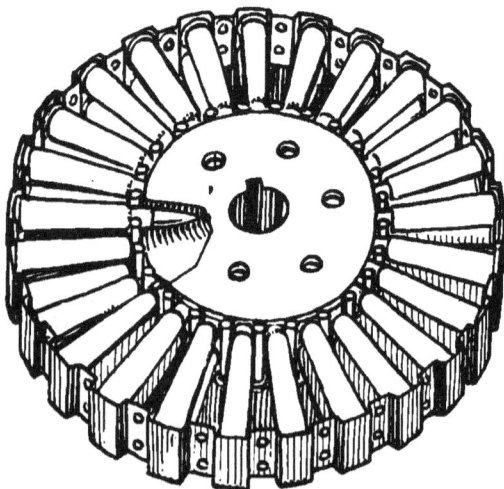

Loaded Magazine.

pegs and the indentations. When the first round is clear of the centre block, it falls on the top of the body, partly by its own weight and helped by the tongue of the body cover. The feed arm moving from right to left and the right side of the cartridge way bearing against the right side of the cartridge,

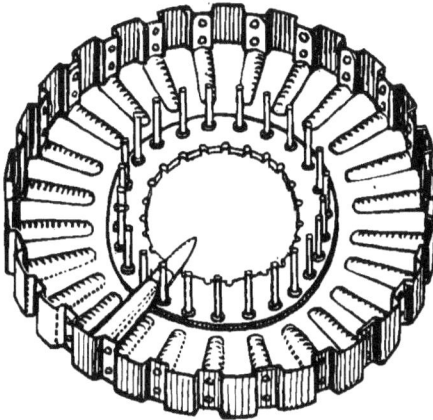

Magazine Minus Centre Block.

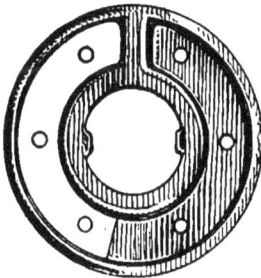

Top View of Centre Block.   Underside View.

the round is carried into the feedway, where it is held in position by the cartridge guide.

The piston rod and bolt continue to travel to the rear until they strike the butt tang, when the force of the gases is expended. If pressure on the trigger is released, the nose of the sear engages the bent in the rack which holds the working parts stationary at the backward position.

THE FORWARD ACTION

WELL, you know something about this already.

> Pressing . . . trigger . . . nose . . . sear
> Becomes disen . . . bent . . . rack.

Remember? It allows the return spring to carry forward the piston rod and bolt. As the bolt travels forward the left side of the striker post bearing against the left curved portion of the cammed slot tries to rotate the bolt but is prevented by the lugs being engaged in the longitudinal guide ways. The nose of the extractor bears against the lower part of the cartridge held in the feedway and carries it forward. The nose of the bullet wants to rise but cannot because of the bullet stop which gives it a forward and downward movement into the chamber. The extractors then grip the rim of the cartridge.

The head of the bullet, striking the head of the ejector, rotates the ejector and causes the tail to swing into the bolt way ready for the next backward movement. As the piston rod and bolt travel forward the boss on the actuating stud, being engaged in the curved tail of the feed arm, causes the feed arm to move from left to right, the feed pawl riding over a corrugation in the magazine and engages behind the corrugation ready for the next backward movement.

At the same time, the feed pawl spring retaining stud rides over the face of the feed stop pawl and depresses it so that the magazine can rotate in the next forward movement.

The piston rod and bolt continue to travel forward until the locking lugs come opposite the locking recesses and then the left side of the striker, by bearing against the left curved portion of the cammed slot, rotates the bolt from left to right and this locks the breach. The striker post continues its journey through the cammed slot, the striker wallops the cap and explodes the charge in the cartridge.

COOLING ACTION

ONE of the principal features of the .303 Lewis is that the rounds which are discharged through the barrel help to keep cool the same barrel that they are responsible for getting so hot. This was the subject of a very slight allusion in the beginning of the book, when we asked you to wait until later before you were told about it.

Here is the way it works:

The gases which are trapped in the gas port follow the bullet out of the barrel—in fact, they are the force which pushes the bullet forward—and when they reach the barrel mouthpiece, they expand into a

fan shape. From there, they strike the forepart of the radiator casing, expelling all the air, and create a vacuum which causes a continuous stream of cool air through the fins of the radiator passing from the rear to the front.

Do you see that the fresh cool air enters the cooling system at the point where the barrel is likely to be hottest, passing towards the muzzle of the barrel where it is not likely to be needed so urgently? It might have been easier to drag the cooling air from the muzzle of the gun towards

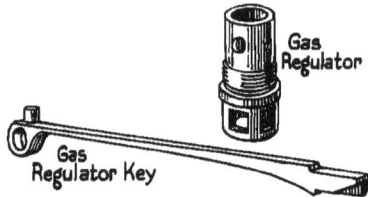

Gas Regulator

Gas Regulator Key

the body. But oh no! The cool air enters the cooling system at the point where it is needed most, and carries on along the barrel to the front through those fins which help to keep it cool.

KEEP IT CLEAN, BROTHER

WHAT's the good of being entrusted with a lovely instrument like the Lewis if it won't ackle the first time you want to use it in serious action?

Quite. So look after it carefully as the racehorse trainer nurtures his stock.

After firing even one round through the barrel, deposits may gather which will cause the gun to fire inaccurately or which may be responsible for a stoppage sufficiently serious to delay you from holding advancing enemy before they have wiped out the greater part of your platoon.

The gunner, therefore, must train himself to have complete confidence in his weapon, and he can do that only by ensuring that it is always clean.

The barrel is liable to suffer from any of three foulings—superficial, internal, or metallic.

Superficial fouling is caused by the waste products of the charge being left on the surface of the bore. This is removed quite simply by the application of the flannelette in the cleaning kit.

Strange as it seems, the steel barrel is porous and each time a round is fired, minute deposits remain on the face of the barrel. They are squashed into the pores of the barrel by the discharge of the bullets which follow. When the barrel cools off, the pores close and imprison these tiny specks of matter, and internal fouling is caused.

The best way to overcome this is to re-heat the barrel by pouring six or eight pints of boiling water down the barrel so that the offending rocks—atoms—can be removed, either by the double pull-through or the cleaning rod.

This boiling water process is necessary after you have fired six hundred rounds or more. Let us hope that you do not have to use the kettle too often.

For cleaning the gas cylinder, a special wire brush and mop are issued. Care should be used to see that all solid foulings are scraped clear of the face of the gas chamber. The wire brush should always be well oiled before using and it should be followed up with the mop.

In cleaning dried oil, rust, etc., from parts of the mechanism, it must be remembered that, although paraffin is a rust remover, it is also a rust creator. Moral: If you have to use paraffin, dry each part thoroughly and oil slightly afterwards.

Metallic fouling is caused by a portion of the nickel envelope of the bullet being left on the face of the lands on the edges of the grooves. Should you notice when inspecting the barrel a whitish streak, the wisest thing you can do is to take the gun to the armourer and tell him you suspect metallic fouling. He'll put it right.

YO-O HEAVE HO

A DOUBLE pull-through is issued with Lewis guns. Similar to the rifle pull-through in some respects, it requires three men to operate it successfully, one on each end and one holding the radiator with both hands. The loop for the 4 by 2 is in the middle, and it is twice as long as the ordinary pull-through. Drop the weight into the barrel from the breach, and while one man holds the barrel firmly the other two continue to pull backwards and forwards with an oily gauze until all rust or fouling is loosened. Next, clean with the cleaning rod and flannelette.

BEFORE, DURING AND AFTER

FIRING

THINK you know all about looking after the gun now? 'Fraid not.

There's a bit more to learn about the attention it needs before you use it, while you are mopping up the advancing foe, and after you have succeeded in maintaining your strong point.

BEFORE.—Dry the bore, oil all frictional parts behind the body locking pin. Test the return spring and adjust if necessary to register at 12 to 14 lbs. In the spare parts bag there is a spring balance. Place one looped end over the cocking handle, pull the cocking handle back, and take the reading. If it is not between the required 12 to 14 lbs., adjust the spring until you have the required tension.

The tension is increased by removing the butt, holding up the pinion group tightly, pulling back the cocking handle two or three inches, releasing the pinion group and allowing it to fall down, and pushing forward the cocking handle until the correct weight is arrived at.

To decrease, drop the pinion group, pull back the cocking handle for two or three inches, hold up the pinion group and connect up.

DURING FIRING.—In a lull, oil frictional parts, special attention being paid to the bolt and striker post. Test the weight of the return spring, replace empty magazines in the carrier and send them back for refilling.

AFTER FIRING.—Reduce the tension to four pounds, oil the barrel and all frictional parts. At the earliest opportunity, strip down and clean as follows: Barrel —thoroughly oil the gauze on the double pull-through. When any fouling of the barrel has been removed by use of the double pull-through, oil the bore with the cleaning rod and wire brush. Clean the gas cylinder with the wire brush and mop.

STOPPAGES

THE gun, set to fire, will continue until A, the pressure on the trigger is released; B, the magazine is empty; or C, some part of the mechanism fails.

Surprisingly, the mechanical failure of the gun is often due to an empty magazine, and the training sequence arranged to detect stoppages, as the mechanical failures are called, incorporates tests to ensure that the gunner is not trying to shoot ammunition which is not there. In fact, most of the stoppages are due to want of care.

Stoppages are described officially as probables and possibles. Probable stoppages are cleared by a set routine which, when accurately applied, will have the gun firing again within four to seven seconds. The routine is called Immediate Action, and will be referred to from now on as I.A. If I.A. does not succeed, secondary action is employed. The I.A. depends on the position of the cocking handle, which will be found in one of three positions—fully forward, over the thumbpiece of the safety catch, or at the rear of the thumbpiece.

With the cocking handle in the first position—fully forward—a stoppage should be dealt with in this order: Attempt to rotate magazine, and, if successful, change, reload and fire. The magazine was empty. If the magazine doesn't rotate, pull back the cocking handle, relay and fire. Probable cause—misfire. If after 1 and 2 the gun still won't fire, change, reload, relay and fire. The magazine was damaged:

Should there still be no response, examine the mechanism in the following order: worn or broken feed pawl or feed pawl spring, worn or broken striker, weak return spring, stop pawl spring broken, gas chamber, gas regulator. Change the broken or weak part, reload, relay and fire.

Cocking handle in *second position*. I.A. pull back, relay and fire. I.A. unsuccessful? Gun firing a few rounds and stopping? Reduce tension by two or three pounds, reload, relay and fire. The probable cause is friction in the working parts. At the first available opportunity the gun should be stripped, cleaned and oiled.

If the stoppage continues in the second position, cock the action, call for the clearing plug, knock back the centre pin, insert in chamber, press the trigger, grip the clearing plug handle, rotate two or three times, pull back the cocking handle and pull out the clearing plug. You will probably find a separated case adhering to the clearing plug. (A " separated case " is due to faulty ammunition and means that the cartridge has broken into two parts.)

THIRD POSITION.—I.A. Pull back, relay and fire. Probable cause is a slight fault in feed. If the gun still will not fire, order " magazine off " and examine the mechanism in the following order: cartridge guide spring may be weak or broken and two rounds will be found on top of the body. This is known as a double feed. Examine chamber to see if the empty case is still there. If so, change the bolt, eject the

case, reload, relay and fire. The cause this time was
a broken extractor. Failing this, feel in the bolt way
with the finger of the right hand for an empty case.
If found, change the ejector, reload, relay and fire.
The trouble here was a broken ejector. If the gun
still doesn't fire, examine the right stop pawl and
magazine for wear or damage.

UNMISTAKABLE STOPPAGES

In addition, there are two unmistakable stoppages.
Where the cocking handle stops in the first position
and the gun fires single shots, immediately change the
left stop pawl. The second shows itself when, on
attempting to pull back the cocking handle, there is
no tension. The return spring has broken and needs
replacing. Some stoppages leave the cocking handle
in either the first or third position. These are due
to one of the following: breakage of the piston rod,
striker post, stop pawl spring, weakness in the return
spring, excessive friction or badly bent magazine.

TRAINING FOR STOPPAGE
DISCOVERY

WHERE it is possible to work under an instructor or as a team, stoppages can be simulated in a variety of ways. The trainee, not knowing what has been done, should go through the immediate and, if necessary, the secondary action to locate the cause. Methods of setting up stoppages are tabulated below and the causes are given in brackets.

Load with dummy and press trigger.
(Misfire.)

Place empty magazine on gun or load magazine with dummy and leave space.
(Empty chamber.)

Remove feed pawl spring.
(Faulty feed pawl on feed pawl spring or damaged magazine.)

Load and press trigger.
(Faulty striker.)

Withdraw cocking handle so that bolt fails to engage behind new round, then push forward slightly.
(Double feed with empty case.)

Depress cartridge nose, advance bolt, and replace magazine.
(Weak cartridge guide spring.)

Load, place empty case in chamber and press
  trigger.
                  (Broken extractor.)

Remove ejector or insert case in ejector way.
                  (Broken ejector.)

THE LEWIS BROTHERS—
.303 AND .300

THE gun we have been describing is the .303. It
has a brother known as the Lewis .300, an American
aircraft weapon and identical in many respects to the
one dealt with in this book.

The fundamental differences between these two
relations are that the .300, being designed for use in
aircraft where there is plenty of air rushing by, the
cooling system is not so elaborate. There is no
aluminium radiator. The feed arm is kept in position at the front of the magazine post by a tongue
instead of a lip. Immediate action is reversed, com-
pared with the instructions given earlier for the .303
because the cocking handle is on the left side. The
sear is actuated by a sear spring and not by a plunger
spring. The gas regulator has four holes instead of
two, and, in addition to the gas chamber, there is
also a gas chamber gland.

However, the .300 weighs about 10 lbs. less than its brother, and the bullet travels faster from the muzzle, although its effective range is only 1,000 yards.

USE YOUR AMMO WISELY

You still need training before you can call yourself a qualified Lewis gunner, because there is plenty to learn about occupying a position without being observed, and drills for the members of the Lewis team which are essential to a group of men who must work in co-ordination.

This book is designed to teach you the fundamentals of the gun. We hope you never have to use it because it is so deadly, but if you do have to, you will find you have a flying start over others who come to it completely ignorant of its killing power and mechanical ingenuity.

KNOW YOUR WEAPONS

No. 2—The ·303 Lewis Gun

The title of this series is self-explanatory. Nor do we think there is any need to stress the usefulness (in fact, the necessity) of it to the general public.

Captain Jacklin, who, with Derek Whipp has compiled the ·303 Lewis gun, was until recently, Small Arms Instructor to the Cripplegate Institute, where his duties included the instruction of Home Guards.

Lastly, it has been the endeavour of the authors and publisher to present this series with the help of diagrams, photographs, etc., in so simple a manner that the information can be readily assimilated by the novice, whilst at the same time it should be of equal value to those who have already had some training in the weapons concerned.

TRAINING MANUALS, TEXT BOOKS AND INSTRUCTIONS

The backbone of all successful armies is its training and tactics. The Naval and Military Press publishes many such manuals of instruction – all perviously long out of print . So, whether your interest lies in the infantry and cavalry tactics of the earliest regiments of the British army in the 18th century, or the weapons manuals and firing instructions of 20th century warfare, the Naval and Military Press has the right book for you.

www.naval-military-press.com

MINES AND BOOBY TRAPS 1943

This is a War Office pamphlet, issued mid-war, in 1943. Its purpose is to introduce sappers to mines commonly used by the British Army – and how to deal with similar devices set by the Germans. The devices described and illustrated cover British anti-tank; grenade; shrapnel and assorted booby trap switches. Enemy mines are covered in chapter 2 with anti-tank, Teller mine types; French anti-tank; Hungarian; anti-personnel German and Italian; and igniters.This is a concise but comprehensive guide for British Army sappers in the art of demining or mine clearance.
9781474539395

THE .303 LEWIS GUN

Illustrated with good clear line drawings this 1941 weapon guide tells the Home Guard Volunteer how to use the 303 Lewis Gun effectively against the invading enemy.A reprint of an original handbook for the .303 Lewis Gun, that was first published in 1941. This book is a practical guide to the handling and maintenance of this iconic weapon.In the crisis following the Fall of France, where a large part of the British Army's equipment had been lost up to and at Dunkirk, stocks of Lewis guns in both .303 and .30-06 were hurriedly pressed back into service, primarily for Home Guard use. Full of fascinating information, this book taught the user the guns capabilities and all he needed to know about maintenance and combat use. Number 2 in the wartime Nicholson & Watson "Know Your Weapons" series, that offer all the important information in a more vivid style than an official publication. Illustrated with good clear line drawings.
9781474539456

ANTI-TANK WEAPONS
Smash The Tank

An insight into the amateur side of World War 2. Diagrams illustrate the main points and the devices, such as the Thermos Bomb;Phosrhorus Bomb;Sticky Bombs; that could be cobbled together from household items are described.This pamphlet was available to the Home Guard and describes the German tank and how to destroy it. It is an early War publication c1940, dealing with the light tanks used by the Germans, also the author gives examples of anti-tank actions in the Spanish Civil War, in which he took part. I'ts is a fascinating look at the "enthusiastic" approach to killing tanks.
9781474539449

TANK HUNTING AND DESTRUCTION 1940

The stated object for the distributing of this War Office manual was as "A guide and help to troops who have the determination and nerve to destroy tanks at close quarters". Intended for fighting on home soil after the very real possibility of a full German invasion, "Operation Sea Lion", this is a remarkable if somewhat naive snap shot of Britain state of preparedness,in her most dangerous hour.
The contents details Tank hunting, Tank characteristics,Tactical action,Road blocks,ambushes Ect,also includes an interesting appendix on Molotov Cocktails, and materials on other ways to destroy tanks.
9781474539401

TROOP TRAINING FOR LIGHT TANK TROOPS NOVEMBER 1939

Very early War tactics pertaining to various aspects of training with and employing armour in the British Army. Covering in concise detail that which a Light tank crew needed to know to be effective in action.
In the early years of the war, Germany held the initiative. German forces used Blitzkrieg tactics in France in 1940, making full use of the speed and armour of tanks to break through enemy defences. It was clear that German tank tactics had evolved during the inter-war period. By contrast, Britain and the Allies were playing catch-up.
9781474539302

JAPANESE WEAPONS ILLUSTRATED
September 1944

This period 'Restricted' laced binding manual was intended to be an aid to the identification of Japanese Army equipment, with sections covering: Tanks, both two-man, Tankette, light and medium; Armoured Cars; Self-Propelled Guns; Anti-Tank Guns; Artillery; Anti-Aircraft Guns; Mortars & Grenade Dischargers; Small Arms; Flamethrowers etc. Produced one year before the surrender of Japan, this work gives a good overview of the weapons the allies would find, fighting an army that despite being on the back foot, was still capable of stiff resistance in an almost entirely defensive role..
9781474539432

NOTES ON THE GERMAN ARMY-WAR
December 1940

An early war 393-page 'Notes' periodical manual from December 1940. It is a detailed review, for use in the field. The manual looks at every aspect of the "Blitzkrieg" German Army (and, to some extent, the Air Force) and gives details as known at the time.

It covers the fighting arms and the services behind them – tactics, organisation, weapons and equipment. It usefully also includes a colour section on uniforms and insignia, a black-and-white plate section of small arms, infantry support and anti-tank weapons, artillery and AFVs. A series of pull-outs related to the text covering tanks etc. are also reproduced.

This is an important first-class picture of the complex fighting machine that was the German Army at the end of the campaigns of 1940, only six months before the invasion of Russia.
9781474539203

GERMAN MINES AND TRAPS

Mid-1940 War Office manual with details of German mines, both the Teller and S-mine (Bouncing Betty) are covered, with techniques for disarming. Good clear full-page line drawings give both practical and technical information. Highly recommended because of the illustrations, which show how these devices worked and the components.
9781474535809

NOTES ON ENEMY ARMY IDENTIFICATIONS ITALY
October 1941

This period handbook was published to give British military personnel a better understanding of the principal characteristics of both the Italian army and the Black Shirt Militia under active service conditions , it is dated October 1941.
It begins with a description of distinctive branches, or specialities, the most characteristic of which was the arm of the Royal Carabinieri, a semi-military body occupying, historically, the senior position in the Army. Other specialities included the Grenadiers of Sardinia, the Bersaglieri, the Alpini and the San Marco Marine Regiment
The handbook then goes on to show, in order, the organisation of Command and Staff, of formations (corps and divisions) and of the arms and services; services, supply and transportation; ranks, plates (many in colour) cover uniforms, insignia, medals and decorations; armament and equipment and a chapter on the Air Force, There are chapters on tactical doctrine and principles of employment, on permanent fortifications, camouflage and abbreviations. Finally there is a brief index.
9781474539746

MANUAL OF GUERILLA TACTICS
Specially Prepared And Based On Lessons From
The Spanish And Russian Campaigns

One of the excellent, concise Bernards Pocket Books, intended to show members of the Home Guard and the regular forces that war is not conducted in a gentlemanly way – it is kill or be killed.
9781474539463

THE OFFENSIVE OF SMALL UNITS
September 1916

This is a periodical tactical manual from 1916, it focuses on the manner in which the French organised and executed their attacks and counterattacks . Summarised from the French, it lays out the process by which to operate in attacks on the German trenches. Focused purely on the operation of infantry, the purpose of this British translation is to give small infantry units the benefit of the French experience in regard to the best methods of combat, in offensive operations.
9781474537971

TRENCH WARFARE
Notes on attack and defence, February 1915

This important period manual was published in early 1915 when hope of a quick ending to the war disappeared, and trench warfare had begun to dominate the Western Front.
The manual strives to instil an offensive spirit and gives practical examples on: Close quarter, local, methods of successful warfare, and German attacks. The salient points to gather were preparation and co-operation between artillery and infantry, and that the capture of trenches is easier than their retention. Two plates illustrating tactics complete this official publication.
9781474539807

Ministry Of Home Security
OBJECTS DROPPED FROM THE AIR 1941

An illustrated Official and confidential publication, covering the many and varied types of objects that were falling from principally German aircraft during the Second phase of the blitz, including high explosives,incendiary bombs and small arms ammunition. Complete with 8 page addendum.
9781783319541

THE MUSKETRY INSTRUCTIONS
FOR THE GERMAN INFANTRY 1887
(Schiessvorshrift fur die Infanterie)
Translated for the intelligence Division War Office

Translated for the War Office by Colonel C W Bowdler Bell

A facsimile that includes the supplement for the German Infantry for 1887. Musketry exercises were intended to give the infantry instruction in shooting, to make effective use of their firearm in battle. As such the manual shows important details designed to make the infantry soldier battle-ready by the end of his first year of service. Instruction is subdivided into Preparatory exercises; Target practice; Field firing; Instructional firing; Inspection in musketry; Proving the rifle M/61.84 and revolver M/83. Many black powder weapons were still used, mainly for training purposes, up to end of the First World War.
9781783313631